Dear Parents and Educators,

Welcome to Penguin Young Readers! As parents and educators, you know that each child develops at their own pace—in terms of speech, critical thinking, and, of course, reading. Penguin Young Readers recognizes this fact. As a result, each Penguin Young Readers book is assigned a traditional easy-to-read level (1–4) as well as an F&P Text Level (A–P). Both of these systems will help you choose the right book for your child. Please refer to the back of each book for specific leveling information. Penguin Young Readers features esteemed authors and illustrators, stories about favorite characters, fascinating nonfiction, and more!

Are Unicorns Real?

LEVEL **4**

F&P TEXT LEVEL **R**

This book is perfect for a **Fluent Reader** who:
- can read the text quickly with minimal effort;
- has good comprehension skills;
- can self-correct (can recognize when something doesn't sound right); and
- can read aloud smoothly and with expression.

Here are some **activities** you can do during and after reading this book:
- Comprehension: After reading the book, answer the following questions:
  - Which animal is sometimes called "the unicorn of the sea"?
  - Which country has the unicorn as its national animal?
  - What type of cattle have the longest and heaviest horns in the world?
- Nonfiction: Nonfiction books deal with facts and events that are real. Talk about the elements of nonfiction. Discuss some of the facts you learned about unicorns. Then, on a separate sheet of paper, write down facts about your favorite unicorns from this book.

Remember, sharing the love of reading with a child is the best gift you can give!

*This book has been officially leveled by using the F&P Text Level Gradient™ leveling system.

For my nieces Hannah and Sarah, Maya
and Liliana, and Lydia, plus nephews Noah
and Tristen: to celebrate the unicorn
inside each of you—GLC

PENGUIN YOUNG READERS
An Imprint of Penguin Random House LLC, New York

Photo credits: used throughout: (frames): subjug/E+/Getty Images Plus; cover, 3: Jennifer Santolla/
Alamy Stock Photo; 4: MadKruben/iStock/Getty Images Plus; 4–5: (background clouds) Gary Yeowell/
DigitalVision/Getty Images Plus, (background tree) Pakin Songmor/Moment/Getty Images Plus;
5: karambol/iStock/Getty Images Plus; 6: Chinnasorn Pangcharoen/iStock/Getty Images Plus; 7:
wichypong/iStock/Getty Images Plus; 8: (from *Christian Topography* by Cosmas Indicopleustes) public
domain, via The Tertullian Project; 9: (mosaic from San Giovanni Evangelista) public domain, via
Wikimedia Commons; 10: ("Virgin and Unicorn" by Domenichino) public domain, via Wikimedia
Commons; 11: (from the Unicorn Tapestries) public domain, via the Metropolitan Museum of Art
(CC0 1.0); 12: gegeonline/iStock/Getty Images Plus; 13: (statue) JohnFScott/iStock/Getty Images Plus,
(ship) Gannet77/iStock/Getty Images Plus, (coin) Caymia/iStock/Getty Images Plus; 14: (Marco Polo)
Grafissimo/DigitalVision Vectors/Getty Images Plus, (Leonardo da Vinci) ivan-96/E+/Getty Images
Plus; 15: Album/Alamy Stock Photo; 16: WILDLIFE GmbH/Alamy Stock Photo; 17: James Warwick/
The Image Bank/Getty Images Plus; 18–19: ДиБгд via Wikimedia Commons (CC BY-SA 4.0); 20: Xi
Zhinong/Nature Picture Library/Alamy Stock Photo; 21: PytyCzech/iStock/Getty Images Plus; 22:
NNehring/E+/Getty Images Plus; 23: Silviculture via Wikimedia Commons (CC BY-SA 3.0); 24–25: VW
Pics/Universal Images Group/Getty Images Plus; 26: DEA/A. DAGLI ORTI/De Agostini/Getty Images
Plus; 27: INTERFOTO/Alamy Stock Photo; 28: Charlotte Bleijenberg/iStock/Getty Images Plus; 29:
WaterFrame_fur/WaterFrame/Alamy Stock Photo; 30: CathyKeifer/iStock/Getty Images Plus; 31:
Marius Faust/EyeEm/Getty Images Plus; 32: nicoolay/iStock/Getty Images Plus; 33: anankkml/iStock/
Getty Images Plus; 34: Dove, W.F. "Artificial production of the fabulous unicorn," *Science Monthly* 42
(1936); 35: Central Historic Books/Alamy Stock Photo; 36–37: Yvonne Hemsey/Hulton Archive/Getty
Images Plus; 38: Photos.com/Getty Images Plus; 39: (from *Protogaea* by Gottfried Wilhelm Leibniz)
public domain, via Wikimedia Commons; 40, 41: Henry Nicholls/SWNS; 42: (top) IraPolyakova/
Shutterstock, (middle) veseba/Shutterstock, (bottom) Ondrej Prosicky/Shutterstock; 43: CARLO
FERRARO/ANSA/EPA; 44: angelinast/iStock/Getty Images Plus; 44–45: (background and Monoceros)
Jazziell/iStock/Getty Images Plus; 46–47: Lisa5201/E+/Getty Images Plus; 48: Demidova_Liliia

Visit us online at www.penguinrandomhouse.com.

Library of Congress Cataloging-in-Publication Data is available upon request.

ISBN 9780593093139 (pbk)   10 9 8 7 6 5 4 3 2 1
ISBN 9780593093146 (hc)   10 9 8 7 6 5 4 3 2 1

PENGUIN YOUNG READERS

LEVEL
4
FLUENT
READER

ARE UNICORNS REAL?

by Ginjer L. Clarke

What Is a Unicorn?

A unicorn is a beautiful white horse with a long horn on its forehead. Or is it? The word *unicorn* literally means "one horn." So other animals with one middle horn are unicorns, too.

In Spanish the word for unicorn is *unicornio,* in French it is *licorne,* and in

German it is *einhorn*. People
have many words for a unicorn.
They also have different ideas
about what a unicorn looks like.

People around the world have told stories about unicorns for thousands of years. The peaceful white unicorn comes from Europe. But the *karkadann* (say: CAR-cuh-din) from the Middle East was loud and scary, with a black horn. Yikes!

The Chinese *ki-lin* was very colorful. It had rainbow scales, a golden mane, and a silver horn! The Japanese *kirin* was a fierce lion with a short, stubby horn.

Unicorn Stories and Art

One of the first unicorn stories was written by a Greek doctor more than 2,000 years ago. He told of a one-horned creature that lived in India. This animal was imaginary, but it was a cross between the body of a rhinoceros and the horn of an antelope.

Later writers told this same story,
but they added details like elephant feet,
a goat beard, or red fur. Oh my! Each
creature had only one horn, so it was
always called a *monoceros*—the Greek
word for "one-horned."

Hundreds of years later, unicorns were part of early Christian Bible stories. Some people thought the unicorn represented Jesus. He was believed to be strong, peaceful, and special—like a unicorn.

Artists during this time created unicorns in many types of art, including tapestries, which are large wall hangings for castles. The most famous of these is a group of tapestries called *The Hunt of the Unicorn.*

The unicorn has a long history in Scotland. It was first included almost 1,000 years ago on the royal coat of arms—an image that represents a family or country. Later, Scottish gold coins had a unicorn on one side.

Today, unicorns can be seen all over Scotland as fountains and statues, and on the HMS *Unicorn*, a nearly 200-year-old wooden ship. National Unicorn Day is April 9. The unicorn is even Scotland's national animal. Cool!

Travelers throughout history, including Marco Polo and Leonardo da Vinci, wrote about the unicorn. But they had never seen one. They were amazed by tales of its special horn.

Marco Polo

Leonardo da Vinci

Most people believed that the
unicorn's horn was not just beautiful—
it was magical! They drank out of
cups made from unicorn horns to
cure diseases. They used unicorn horn
powder to protect against poisoned food.

But were these real unicorn horns?

Unicorn Look-Alikes

The horns that people believed came from unicorns were often really from the Indian rhinoceros. The word *rhinoceros* means "nose horn."

A rhino's horn is made of the same material as your fingernails and hair. Wow! The horn grows as the rhino gets older. It can grow to be two feet long.

Rhino horn was used in medicine. It was also made into buckles, buttons, cups, knife handles, and more.

Long ago, there lived a giant one-horned creature much larger and furrier than today's rhino. *Elasmotherium* (say: uh-LAZZ-muh-theer-ee-um) is called the Siberian unicorn.

Scientists once believed that the Siberian unicorn went extinct about

200,000 years ago. But in 2016, a fossil was found that proves this unicorn still roamed the earth during the last Ice Age—only 30,000 years ago.

This animal may have been the true unicorn in ancient stories!

Another creature that may have inspired unicorn tales is the chiru (say: CHEER-oo), or Tibetan antelope. The chiru has super-long, twisted black horns. When seen from the side, the chiru appears to have only one horn—like a unicorn.

The Arabian oryx (say: OR-icks) has long horns, too. Early Egyptian people sometimes painted the oryx as it looked from the side. This may have added to the idea that it was a unicorn. Weird!

The okapi (say: oh-COP-ee) is funny looking! It has zebra-striped legs on a horse body. It has big ears and short horns on its head, like a giraffe. The okapi is rare and hard to find, so it is called the African unicorn.

The saola (say: SOW-luh), or Asian unicorn, is one of the world's rarest large mammals. It was only discovered less than 30 years ago. Scientists believe at most a few hundred of these super-shy forest creatures still exist.

Real-Life Unicorns

The narwhal is also rare and shy. It is called "the unicorn of the sea." But the male narwhal's long, twisted tusk is not a horn on its head. It is a tooth growing out of its top lip! This amazing tooth can be up to 10 feet long. Whoa!

Scientists used to think that the male narwhal's tusk only had a few uses, like fighting other males and impressing females. But not long ago they discovered that a narwhal can also "taste" how salty and cold the ocean water is through its sensitive tooth.

For a long time, many people thought narwhal tusks were unicorn horns. They had never seen a narwhal, but the tusks were sold in Europe by whale hunters. They believed the tusks had healing powers.

Narwhal tusks were expensive and collected by royal families. Some tusks were made into furniture, treasures, and even "unicorn thrones." Wild!

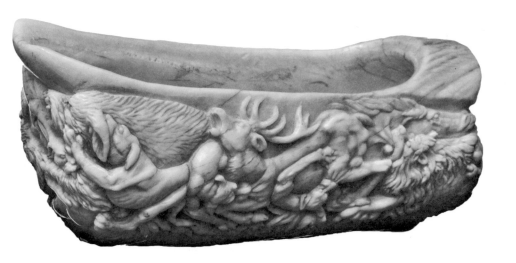

Some other sea creatures are unicorns, too. The unicornfish has a horn-like spike on its forehead. This horn grows as the fish gets older. The horn gets so long that an adult unicornfish cannot reach its food and has to change the way it eats.

A unicorn shrimp has a long red spike between its eyes. The shrimp's horn is covered in tiny teeth and can be used like a spear to catch prey. Gotcha!

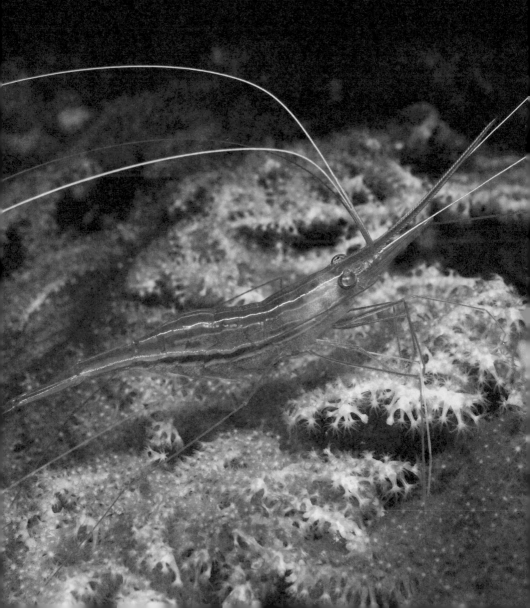

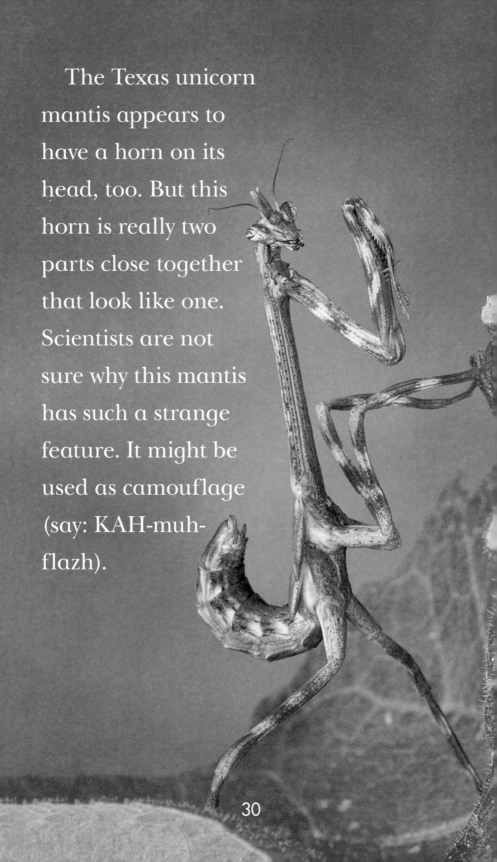

The Texas unicorn mantis appears to have a horn on its head, too. But this horn is really two parts close together that look like one. Scientists are not sure why this mantis has such a strange feature. It might be used as camouflage (say: KAH-muh-flazh).

A male rhinoceros beetle uses its large, curved horn like a shovel. It scoops or pushes another male out of the way during a battle. Epic!

Wannabe Unicorns

The aurochs (say: OR-ocks) was a huge, hairy ox that lived long ago. This ox may actually be the animal the Bible said was a unicorn. Its name got mixed up when the stories were translated from one language into another. Oops!

Watusi cattle in Africa have the longest and heaviest horns in the world. Herders of these cattle used to turn a baby bull, a male cow, into a unicorn by training its huge horns to grow together. The unicorn bull became the leader of its herd.

A man named Dr. Dove learned about the tradition of unicorn bulls. He wanted to make his own. In 1933, he created the first one-horned bull in the United States. He said that his unicorn bull was strong but gentle.

Before that, some sheep from Nepal were taken to England in 1906. They were a gift to the Prince of Wales. Some of these sheep had three or four horns, instead of two. But a couple had only one big horn—unicorn sheep!

In the 1980s, a man named Oberon Zell continued Dr. Dove's idea. He tried gently twisting the small horns of a young goat together, among other means. The goat's two horns would slowly grow into one, making it a unicorn.

Zell made several unicorn goats and sold one to a circus. They called him Lancelot the Living Unicorn. Some people thought Lancelot's big horn was fake. But when the circus proved it was real, this cute goat became famous!

A German scientist named Otto von Guericke did not make a living unicorn. He made up a dead one!

In 1663, some bones were found in a cave in Germany. Dr. von Guericke decided the bones came from a unicorn.

He put the bones together into a
unicorn shape and included
a drawing of it in a book.

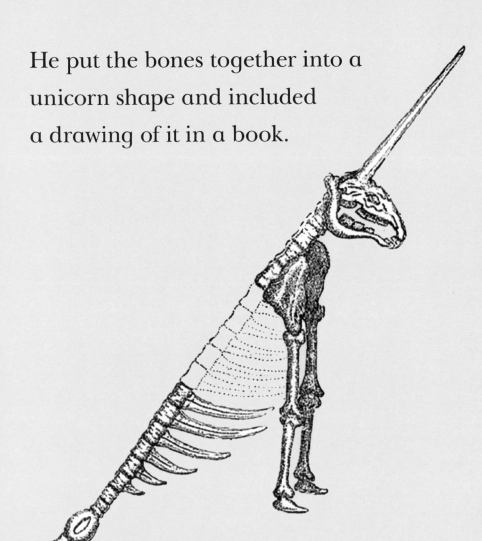

Some people thought this skeleton was
proof that unicorns existed. The skeleton
is still displayed in a German museum.
It looks pretty silly today. What do
you think?

Finding Unicorns

Some unicorns were created by people on purpose, but one famous unicorn animal was made by mistake.

In 2016, some kids on a field trip at a farm in England pulled on the horn of a sheep named Peanut. The horn broke off! Peanut was not hurt, but now she is a "ewenicorn"—a ewe is a female sheep. Ha-ha!

Other unicorn animals just occur naturally. These different types of antelopes all have only one horn—by birth or sometimes from fights.

This small unicorn deer was found in 2008 in a nature park in Italy. He was born with only one horn, but his twin brother had the normal two horns!

Many people believed that the stories of magical unicorns were real until about 200 years ago. Eventually, most people decided unicorns were only make-believe. But some people are still searching. Are you?

One place where a unicorn can always be found is surprising—in the sky! The constellation, or cluster of stars, called Monoceros is near the constellation of Orion the Hunter. Maybe he is looking for unicorns, too!

Orion constellation

Monoceros constellation

The unicorn of myths may never have existed. Or perhaps it was once real, but not as we imagine it today.

"Being a unicorn" has also come to mean loving whatever makes you special. So perhaps unicorns are not found in the forest—but inside of you!

The unicorn has always represented good things many people want—like peace, beauty, and mystery.

Believing in unicorns is now also about believing in yourself and in others. What makes you a unicorn?